THE ISRAELIS
AND
PALESTINIANS

SMALL STEPS TO PEACE

Ted Gottfried

The Millbrook Press
Brookfield, Connecticut

Published by The Millbrook Press, Inc.
2 Old New Milford Road
Brookfield, Connecticut 06804
www.millbrookpress.com

Library of Congress Cataloging-in-Publication Data
Gottfried, Ted.
The Israelis and Palestinians : small steps to peace / Ted Gottfried.
p. cm. — (Headliners)
Includes bibliographical references (p.) and index.
Summary: Examines the latest developments in the peace process
between Israel and the displaced Palestinians led by Yasir Arafat.
ISBN 0-7613-1859-3 (lib. bdg.)
1. Arab-Israeli conflict—1993—Peace—Juvenile literature.
[1. Arab-Israeli conflict—1993—Peace.] I. Title. II. Series.
DS119.76.G68 2000
956.95'3044—dc21 00-022821

Cover photographs courtesy of © Reuters/Jamal Saidi/Archive and
© Chip Hires/Liaison Agency

Photographs courtesy of © Liaison Agency: pp. 4 (Bryan
McBurney), 10 (right, Chip Hires), 14 (Will Yurman), 16 (right,
Noel Quidu), 27 (Francolon/Haik), 40 (Catherine Leroy), 47, 52
(Will Yurman); © Reuters/Archive Photos: pp. 7 (Jim Hollander),
10 (left, HO), 45 (Jim Hollander); © Hulton Getty/Liaison
Agency: pp. 16 (left), 21, 25; © Archive Photos: pp. 18, 30
(Agence France Presse), 33, 35 (Popperfoto), 38; The Illustrated
London News Picture Library: p. 23; AP/Wide World Photos: pp.
49, 54

Contents

Chapter 1

A New Day Dawns

The little boy wore faded blue jeans with holes in the knees as he ambled past the outdoor café in Jerusalem on a warm May day in 1999. The tourist sipping iced mint tea couldn't tell if the boy was an Israeli Jew or a Palestinian Arab. "Shalom," the tourist greeted the boy. The word meant "peace." The boy smiled. "Barak," he replied, speaking the name of Israel's newly elected prime minister. The smile faded. "Maybe," he added.

Hope and skepticism—this was the mixture of moods among all Israelis and Palestinians in the aftermath of the Israeli election replacing the Likud government of Benjamin Netanyahu with the One Israel party of Ehud Barak. Netanyahu had been opposed to the "land-for-peace" agreements reached with Palestinian leader Yasir Arafat and had kept them from being carried out during the three years he had been prime minister. By contrast,

Opposite:
Young people supporting Ehud Barak's One Israel party wave flags at a rally four days before the May 1999 election in which Barak was chosen to be the new prime minister of Israel.

saying that the "Palestinian state is inevitable," Barak pledged to implement the agreements speedily.

This would not be simple. The conflict between Jews and Palestinians had its roots in centuries-old disputes. These had come to a head in 1948 when the Jews had taken over Palestine and declared that it was now the nation of Israel. Hundreds of thousands of Palestinians had fled to neighboring Arab countries to live in refugee camps set up on the borders with Israel. Over the decades that followed—marked by violence and war—the Palestinians had demanded reparations and the reestablishment of the Palestinian nation. Recently there had been meetings held and agreements reached between the Palestinians and Israelis, but very little had actually changed.

Barak had promised action, but he had problems. Thirty-five parties had participated in the election, and fifteen had elected members to the Knesset (the Israeli parliament). The 120 seats had been won not only by Barak and Likud supporters but also by many single-issue parties.

The ultra-Orthodox Shas party, dedicated to imposing Jewish religious law on the nation, came in third in the election, winning seventeen seats. The aims of the Shas were opposed by secular (nonreligious) Israelis, including most Barak backers, as well as the left-wing Meretz party (winner of nine seats), which favored a Palestinian state. The two Russian Israeli parties—Yisrael Ba-aliya and Yisrael Beitinu, with eleven Knesset seats—represented 740,000 recent immigrants. Sephardic (Jews originating in the Arab world) supporters of Shas claimed that the government showed favoritism to the generally better educated and well-off Russians. The Russian parties opposed "land for peace," government restrictions on business, and religious dictates by the Orthodox.

Other parties in the Knesset included the National Religious party, which won five seats, supporting further

West Bank Jewish settlement in violation of agreements reached with the Palestinians, as well as parties backing such diverse issues as a free-market economy, a communist economic policy, separation of church and state, equality for Israeli Arabs, and structural changes in government to eliminate political elites. The Likud, with its nineteen seats, refused to join a coalition led by Barak. To line up the support he needed from these parties to retain control of the Knesset, the new prime minister had to do some quick and fancy juggling before he had the backing to deal with Yasir Arafat.

Israeli soldiers pass election posters showing the Likud candidate, Benjamin Netanyahu (with blue writing), and the Shas candidate, Aryeh Deri, whose posters have been defaced.

Arafat's Situation

Meanwhile, Arafat had troubles of his own. In 1993 and 1996 he had signed the Oslo and Wye peace agreements with the Israelis, only to have the Netanyahu government balk at carrying them out because of continuing Palestinian terrorism. Arafat had been elected president of the new Palestinian National Authority (PNA) by an overwhelming vote and his al-Fatah party controlled its parliament, but his inability to make the Israelis implement the peace accords was causing increasing dissatisfaction among his people. He was accused of overriding his parliament, deliberately postponing the establishment of a constitution, and ruling like a dictator.

There was strong opposition to Arafat by other Palestinian factions. These included Hamas (the Islamic Resistance Movement), led by Sheikh Ahmed Yassin and heavily financed by Iran; the Popular Front for the Liberation of Palestine, which embraced Marxist principles and was headed by Dr. George Habash; the radical Shiite Hezbollah (Party of God) based in Lebanon; and the Palestinian Islamic Jihad, among others. These groups had denounced Arafat for compromising with the Israelis and selling out the Palestinian cause.

Accordingly, they had undermined Arafat with terrorist attacks that crippled the peace agreements. The free clinics and schools they ran for Palestinian refugees earned support at Arafat's expense. They spread "no compromise" propaganda along with a fundamentalist Muslim doctrine encouraging young converts to enlist as suicide bombers.

Under the peace agreements, Palestinian terrorism was to be controlled by Arafat's police. Israelis expected them to nip it in the bud by arresting suspected terrorists. When they did this, the result was to alienate many Arafat supporters. When they failed to do it, Arafat was accused by the Israelis of condoning terrorist acts.

Corruption on Both Sides

Corruption was another major problem in Arafat's administration. He had used government jobs to reward political allies. Members of the police force had extorted money from merchants in exchange for protection. International loans for development projects had been skimmed by government officials for personal gain.

The Israelis were also dealing with corruption scandals. There were charges against former Prime Minister Netanyahu involving repairs done to his private home and billed to the government. The police official heading the investigation received anonymous death threats. At the same time, the conviction of Shas leader Aryeh Deri for corruption was keeping Barak from enlisting Shas in the coalition he had to forge in order to govern. Some were suspicious of Barak's appointment of cabinet ministers because of the business opportunities so often associated with such positions. As the *Jerusalem Post* put it, "When there are spoils to be divided, the good of the country as a whole comes second."

Behind the rough-and-tumble politics, however, there were genuine commitments to the safety of Israel and to peace. Deri resigned from Shas, and Barak was able to form a seven-party coalition that included the ultra-Orthodox party. The cabinet appointed by Barak included former Likud member David Levy as foreign minister with other key posts going to leaders of the parties in the coalition.

A Revised Peace Agreement

Events moved quickly after Barak's inauguration as prime minister on August 3. Pledging to make peace with the Palestinians, Syria, and Lebanon a "supreme goal," he embarked on a series of meetings with President Mubarak of Egypt, King Abdullah of Jordan, President Clinton,

The Cold-Blooded Peacemaker

Israeli prime minister Ehud Barak was born on a kibbutz (communal farm) on February 12, 1942. His father was an orphan whose family had been killed in a pogrom (an organized massacre of Jews) in Lithuania. His mother was a Holocaust survivor whose family was murdered in a Nazi concentration camp. One of four sons, Ehud was a gifted pianist as a boy. He also had a talent for picking locks. This resulted in his being expelled from high school. Nevertheless, he went on to become a physicist.

In the army he met Navah Cohen, a schoolteacher who, like Ehud, was completing the military service required of young Israelis. Navah, of Algerian descent, became Ehud's wife. Married more than thirty years, they have three daughters.

Barak stayed in the military and showed an ability to memorize maps, which enabled him to move through terrain in the dark. He led a secret commando unit operating in Arab territory. Benjamin Netanyahu, who lost the post of prime minister to Barak in the 1999 election, served under him.

Barak led the 1973 rescue of airliner hostages held by Arab insurgents. He commanded a successful raid to kidnap five Syrian officers from Lebanon. He put on a wig and a dress and led a mission into Beirut to assassinate three terrorist leaders. The most decorated soldier in the history of the Israeli Army, Barak gained a reputation for ruthlessness and having "the blood of a lizard."

In 1991, Barak became Chief of Staff of the Israeli Army. He left the army in 1995 to serve as Interior Minister in the Labor party government headed by Yitzhak Rabin. After Rabin was assassinated in 1995, he became foreign minister. In June 1997 he was elected chairman of the Labor party. Two years later, running on a peace platform, Ehud Barak scored a landslide victory to become prime minister of Israel.

Ehud Barak as a soldier in 1970

Ehud Barak as a politician in 1999

and Arafat. He then proposed talks with the Syrians and the Lebanese to set a fifteen-month deadline to achieve peace in the Middle East. By including the Palestinians in this deadline, Barak was in effect asking for a postponement in the carrying out of the Wye Accords, which Netanyahu had agreed to, but then balked at carrying out. The Wye Accords had called for turning over 13 percent of the West Bank to Palestinian control in three stages. Barak had pledged to carry out the Wye Accords, but was faced with protests that the third withdrawal would leave fifteen Jewish settlements surrounded by Palestinian areas. He was trying to defuse opposition to this by members of his Knesset coalition.

Arafat declared the fifteen-month deadline "unacceptable." He demanded the turnover of the areas agreed to at Wye. Anti-Arafat Palestinian groups based in Syria and Jordan vowed to "continue to fight Israel." Hamas threatened more jihad (holy war) operations and suicide bombings inside Israel.

Barak met with Arafat to allay concerns that he might give priority to peace with Syria while delaying the turning over of West Bank territory. The Israelis suspended financing for construction of new Israeli factories in the West Bank and Gaza Strip, projects opposed by the Palestinians. A promise was made to halt the new Jewish settlement activity in occupied areas begun under Netanyahu. Israeli soldiers ousted new settlers from mobile homes on the West Bank.

After more than a month of tension during which Barak and Arafat jockeyed for position, a revised peace schedule was reached at the beginning of September 1999. A target date of September 2000 was set for a final peace agreement. However, coalition approval of the agreement was threatened by a confrontation between Shas and Israeli minister of education Yossi Sharad, leader of the secular Meretz party. Sharad was withholding funds from Shas-run religious schools on the grounds

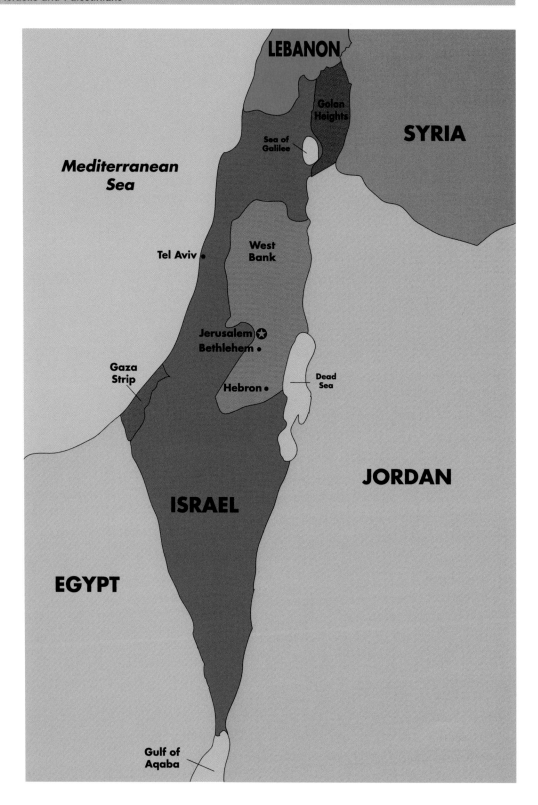

that the money was being mismanaged. Shas was threatening to quit Barak's coalition and leave him without a majority in the Knesset. The standoff was resolved when some money was released to Shas, and they withdrew their threat to leave the coalition. However, it was a threat that would continue to be made.

Roadblocks and Hope

Barak was also trying to deal with Lebanon, where approximately 350,000 Palestinian refugees lived in squalid camps on the Israeli border. This could only be done by dealing with Syria as well. Since the end of World War I, when the victors carved up what had been the Turkish Ottoman Empire, Syrians had considered Lebanon a territory stolen from Syria. When civil war broke out in Lebanon in 1976, Syria sent in a 35,000-man army to restore the peace. The Syrians have controlled Lebanon ever since.

Frequent attacks across the Lebanese border by Palestinian guerrillas had been blamed on Syria by Israel. Reprisals included bombings of the refugee camps by Israeli planes and raids on them by Lebanese Phalangists—Christian militia allied with the Israelis. By 1999 the Israeli Army and the Phalangists occupied 10 percent of Lebanese territory, a "security zone" across from the Palestinian camps.

Barak announced his intention to withdraw Israeli forces from the security zone. However, Lebanon cannot make peace with Israel without Syria's consent. That consent hinges on Israel giving back the Golan Heights (an area seized during the 1967 Six-Day War) to Syria. Complicating matters is a July 1999 report by an organization called Human Rights Watch, which found that in the Lebanese territory held by Israel, local citizens were being expelled and threatened with death if they returned. Israel denied the charges.

Palestinian refugee children in Beirut, Lebanon

Even as Israel, Syria, and Lebanon were probing the possibilities of peace, the radical Shiite party Hezbollah continued to be a major roadblock. Financed by Iran, Hezbollah fired rockets across the border killing several Israelis and attacked a Phalangist force inside the security zone. When Arafat met with various PLO leaders to try to persuade them to accept the revised peace agreements, Hezbollah leader Sheikh Hassan Nasrallah condemned them for meeting with a "cowardly traitor."

Hezbollah was not alone in opposing the quest for peace with increased violence. Other terrorist attacks on Israelis also undermined the peace process. On the road halfway between Jerusalem and Tel Aviv, a Palestinian twice plowed his car into Israeli soldiers, injuring eleven of them. Drive-by shootings on the West Bank injured Jewish settlers. Haifa was shaken by a bomb being transported by an Israeli Palestinian. In Tiberias, two other Israeli Palestinians set off a bomb, killing themselves and seriously wounding an Israeli Jewish woman.

At the same time the opportunity to achieve a lasting peace was greater than it had ever been. Leaders of Arab countries were negotiating with an Israeli leader. Anti-PLO leaders were softening toward Arafat. The Israel Defense Force was planning a unilateral withdrawal of Israeli forces from the Lebanese security zone, anticipating a peace treaty to be reached with the governments of Syria and/or Lebanon.

The new peace schedule was being implemented. The first transfers of land to the Palestinian National Authority were made; and 350 Palestinian prisoners were released. A "safe passage" route for Palestinians was established between the Gaza Strip and the West Bank. For many in Gaza it meant a chance to get jobs, as well as a chance to reconnect with relatives they had not seen during the long years that the Israeli authorities had forbidden such travel. For both Israelis and

First Palestinian President

Born in Jerusalem in 1929, Yasir Arafat was raised in Cairo, Egypt. At age seventeen he smuggled weapons from Egypt to the Palestinians. When the nation of Israel was established in 1948, he vowed to devote his life to reclaiming the Palestinian homeland. He joined the Egyptian Army and studied guerrilla tactics. After leaving the army, he led raids into Israel. This led Egyptian president Gamal Nasser to banish him.

Arafat went to Tunisia, where he set up a worldwide network to raise money for the Palestinian cause. In 1959 he organized al-Fatah, the largest Palestinian insurgency force. In 1964 the Palestine Liberation Organization (PLO) was formed as a political wing of al-Fatah with Arafat as its leader.

After the 1967 war, Arafat's PLO moved to Jordan. In 1970 they fought a bloody war against the Jordanian Army, were defeated, and fled to Lebanon. In 1974 the Arab nations recognized the PLO "as the sole legitimate representative of the Palestinian people." Eight years later an Israeli invasion forced the PLO to flee Lebanon.

In November 1988, Arafat declared Palestine an independent state. Then, despite opposition from hard-liners, Arafat affirmed "the right" of Palestine, Israel, and their neighbors "to exist in peace and security." In the early 1990s, secret talks with the Israelis resulted in the 1993 Oslo Accords, establishing a timetable for Palestinian self-rule. However, when implementation was delayed, militants demanded that Palestinians "revolt against Arafat."

Arafat was elected first president of the Palestinian National Authority in 1996, receiving 88 percent of the votes cast. Still, his authority is constantly challenged by die-hard Palestinian factions and fundamentalist Muslim clergy. Today, although ailing and no longer young, Arafat remains the living symbol of the Palestinian cause.

Yasir Arafat as a young Palestinian resistance leader in 1953

Yasir Arafat as leader of the Palestinian Liberation Organization (PLO) in 1999

Palestinians, for the first time in their many centuries of common history, there was a real chance of peace for the coming millennium.

As in the past, however, the road to peace would be filled with violent, and often confusing, detours. Mistrust between Israelis and Palestinians would not easily be overcome. Intentions would be misinterpreted and words misconstrued. Also, Israelis would disagree with Israelis, Palestinians with Palestinians; groups on both sides would break off and declare their own agendas and their own, sometimes violent, methods; and other nations with other objectives would interfere, take sides, and incite aggression. Distinguishing among the various groups and individuals, and understanding their motives and goals, can be confusing. The aim of this book is to help clarify that confusion and to explain its effect on the quest for peace.

Chapter 2

A History of Two Peoples

Palestine is the Middle East region between the Jordan River and the Mediterranean Sea. Today the region is a part of Israel. Originally it was settled by an ancient tribe of farmers called Canaanites. Hebrew tribes arrived around 1500 B.C. In 1000 B.C., they formed a kingdom that later split into two states, Israel and Judah. This would be the basis for later claims to the land by Zionists (those who believed in establishing a Jewish homeland).

Before the birth of Christ the region was conquered by a series of foreign powers including Assyria, Babylonia, the Persians, Alexander the Great, the Egyptians, and—finally—the Romans. Under the rule of the Roman Empire, the Jews were reduced to a slave population. They rebelled, and in A.D. 70 the Romans destroyed Jerusalem, the holiest city of the Jews. In A.D. 132 the Romans killed more than half a million Jewish men in more than one thousand villages.

Opposite: The Prophet Muhammad, founder of Islam, the religion that came to dominate this area of the Middle East

Between A.D. 1 and 500, non-Jewish Palestinians came to consider themselves part of a wider Arabic civilization. At the same time, many embraced Christianity. By the seventh century, Christians formed the majority of the Palestinian population.

In 613 the Prophet Muhammad began preaching the new religion of Islam. His followers called themselves Muslims. The Arab conquest of Palestine in 641 drove out the Romans and introduced Islam to the country. By the tenth century, most Palestinians had converted to Islam. Defections from Christianity provided one of the excuses for the Crusades, which began in the eleventh century. In 1099 the Crusaders seized Jerusalem and established a kingdom in Palestine.

During the Arab conquest of 641, Jews had begun to leave Palestine in large numbers. Now the anti-Semitic rampages of the Crusaders turned their exodus into a stampede. The Jews would disperse over many countries of Europe, a phenomenon known as the Diaspora.

Initially, the Jews fled to Spain. They lived there peacefully until the Spanish Inquisition, when they were presented with the choice of either converting to Catholicism or being burned at the stake. They then fled to Italy, France, and Germany. In the fifteenth and sixteenth centuries they were banished from Spain, France, and Portugal. They were driven from Germany by pogroms and fled to Poland. Eventually, anti-Semitism spread over all of Eastern Europe, including Russia, and Jews were relegated to ghettos and persecuted in a variety of ways up to and including the twentieth century.

The Birth of Zionism

Meanwhile, the Crusaders had been driven out of Palestine by the Mamelukes of Egypt, and the Mamelukes in turn were expelled by armies of the

Turkish Ottoman Empire in the seventeenth century. Palestine was still occupied and ruled by Turkey at the end of the nineteenth century, when small numbers of Jews began returning. They were sponsored by Baron Edmond Rothschild, a wealthy French Jew. He acted out of concern for persecuted European Jews, but also regarded financing them as an investment. His funds "drained swamps, dug wells, ploughed land, built houses, surveyed terrains." However, before long, Baron Rothschild began laying down rules and dictating what should be done with the profits generated by the colonists. He insisted that "these are *my* colonies, and I shall do with them as I like."

Theodor Herzl was born in Budapest, now the capital of Hungary, in 1860. He was a journalist who, after witnessing an anti-Semitic riot in Paris, decided to devote his work to establishing a Jewish homeland.

Then, in 1897, the First Zionist Congress convened in Basel, Switzerland. So began the movement to establish a Jewish homeland in Palestine. The movement grew slowly until 1903, when a vicious anti-Semitic book called *The Protocols of the Learned Elders of Zion* was published. Using forged documents, *The Protocols* claimed to expose a Jewish plot to conquer the world and enslave Christians. Circulated throughout Europe, *The Protocols* generated a wave of anti-Semitism. This energized the Zionist movement and spurred emigration to Palestine.

During the early 1900s, the Jewish population in Palestine rose to 60,000. In 1918 the majority population of Palestinian Arabs consisted of 500,000 Muslims and 100,000 Christians. The British had driven the Turks out of Palestine during World War I. The Arabs had been led to believe that the British would create an independent Arab state that would include Palestine. In 1917, however, the British government issued the Balfour Declaration, which supported Zionism. Arab Palestinians feared being overwhelmed by waves of Jewish immigrants. In 1922 the League of Nations approved British rule over Palestine. Throughout the 1920s, however, Jewish settlements in Palestine came under attack.

The White Paper

Adolf Hitler and the Nazis came to power in Germany in 1933. Anti-Semitism was key to their program. Many Jews fled Europe for Palestine. By 1939, there were 400,000 Jews in Palestine, and they made up more than a third of the area's population. In 1936 the Arab Committee had been formed to oppose Jewish purchases of Palestinian land and to fight Jewish emigration to Palestine. It was headed by the Grand Mufti of Jerusalem. For the next three years the Grand Mufti led a civil war against British rule and Jewish immigration. Thousands of people were killed.

To stop the violence, Great Britain issued a White Paper in 1939 guaranteeing the establishment of an independent Palestine with an Arab majority within ten years. Jewish immigration was to be limited to 1,500 a month until 1944, when it was to be stopped altogether. With the rest of the world already closing its doors to Jewish refugees, the White Paper was virtually a death sentence for the Jews of Europe.

Millions of Jews were killed in the Holocaust during World War II. The British helped to fight those who were slaughtering the Jews. In 1940 a force of 90,000 Palestinian Jews fought beside the British. By 1944, however, with the British blocking further Jewish emigration to Palestine, militant Zionists slipped into Cairo and assassinated Lord Moyne, the British resident minister for the Middle East.

The Grand Mufti of Jerusalem

The Holocaust

In September 1941 a German police battalion and a Ukrainian *Schutzmannschaft* (police force) came to Babi Yar in the Ukraine. They herded small groups of Jews—men, women, and children—to the edge of a ravine and machine-gunned them. The bodies fell backward into the ravine. The massacre lasted two days. When it was over, 33,000 Jews were dead.

This was only one of the mass shootings of European Jews between 1939 and 1945. However, most of those slaughtered during World War II died not by shooting but in Nazi death camp gas chambers. Six million Jewish men, women, and children were murdered. Two thirds of the Jews of Europe died. The Holocaust wiped out one of every three Jews in the world.

Recently, some doubts have been expressed as to the reality of the Holocaust. Yet few events in history have been as well documented. There are hundreds of carefully kept Nazi records, as well as forty-two volumes of trial evidence filled with the testimony of eyewitnesses—many of them German—confirming the full extent of the Holocaust. There are also so-called Death Books containing records of mass murders of Jews kept by those in charge of carrying them out. There are signed extermination orders, boastful reports of increases in killings, transportation records of the millions delivered to their death, bills for the gas used to kill them, even films taken by the Nazis of the murders.

The evidence is not only overwhelming, it is beyond doubt.

Crisis of the DPs

In the aftermath of the war, weak and sick Jews who had survived Nazi concentration camps were put in Displaced Persons (DP) camps with Poles, Ukrainians, Germans, Latvians, Hungarians, Croats, and others, many of whom were anti-Semitic. They often met with persecution and violence. Meanwhile, a debate was going on in the newly formed United Nations. The Russians insisted that refugees either wanted to go back to their homelands "or were traitors, war criminals, or collaborators." Representing the United States, Eleanor Roosevelt, the world-renowned wife of the late president Franklin

Delano Roosevelt, opposed forcing DPs to return to places where their lives were at risk. For example, in July 1946 twenty-six Jews who had returned to Kielce, Poland, were killed in a pogrom. Mrs. Roosevelt's view prevailed, and Jewish DPs were given a choice about where to settle.

Desperate to get to Palestine, Jewish displaced persons (DPs) often endured cramped conditions aboard the ships that would take them there.

Most Jewish DPs wanted to go to Palestine, but the British continued to restrict immigration. Defying the restrictions, young Jews ran the blockade in old and sometimes leaky ships to bring DPs to Israel. The British sometimes fired on these vessels. More often they captured them and placed the DPs in internment camps in Cyprus. However, many DPs made it through. The British staged periodic raids to round them up. The DPs were held behind barbed wire before being deported. In August 1946 a crowd of Palestinian Jews stormed Haifa's barbed-wire port area as the illegals were being loaded for deportation. British soldiers opened fire and killed three people. As the crowd was turned back, the DPs marching up the gangplank of the ship taking them from Palestine sang the Jewish anthem "Hatikvah," which in English means hope.

One ship, the *Exodus,* sailed from France carrying 4,530 Jews who were almost all originally from Germany. It was intercepted by the British, who forced it to go to Hamburg, where the Jews were forced to disembark. The German Jews were back in the country where the Holocaust had begun.

The Seeds of Jihad

In November 1947 the United Nations voted to split Palestine into Arab and Jewish states. The Palestinians protested giving up any part of their territory. Nevertheless, the British prepared to move their forces out. Chaos followed. Violence increased between Jews and Palestinians. In the wake of a massacre at the Arab village of Deir Yasin, many Palestinians fled their homeland.

On May 14, 1948, Prime Minister David Ben-Gurion proclaimed the establishment of the independent state of Israel. The violence escalated. Armies from Jordan,

Prime Minister David Ben-Gurion proclaims the establishment of Israel on
May 14, 1948. Above him hangs a portrait of Theodor Herzl.

Massacre at Deir Yasin

In the spring of 1948, Deir Yasin was a Palestinian village of seven hundred people. With Arab-Jewish violence mounting, Deir Yasin signed a nonaggression pact with an adjacent Jewish community. Deir Yasin denied the Arab Liberation Army permission to use their village as a base. The people of Deir Yasin wanted peace. On April 9, 1948, that hope was shattered by the Irgun, a commando unit operating independently of the Haganah, the official Zionist militia.

The villagers were awakened by a loudspeaker giving them fifteen minutes to leave their town. When the deadline wasn't met, there was a skirmish. By noon the next day, the fighting was over, and the village was calm. Haganah Colonel Meir Pa'el describes what he observed then:

"The Irgun . . . shot whoever they saw, women and children included. The commanders did not try to stop the massacre. . . . I pleaded with the commander to order his men to cease fire, but to no avail. In the meantime 25 Arabs had been loaded on a truck . . . taken to the quarry . . . and murdered in cold blood."

The Irgun tossed some of the bodies in the village well to poison the water. They paraded some 150 captured women and children through the streets of Jerusalem. Altogether, 254 people—old men, women, and children—were slaughtered and 300 others wounded.

The massacre's effect on the Palestinians' attitude toward Israelis is summed up in this poem by Tewfiq Zayad:

> And in your throat we shall stay,
> A piece of glass,
> A cactus thorn,
> And in your eyes,
> A blazing fire.

Egypt, Lebanon, Syria, and Iraq came to the aid of the Palestinians and invaded Israel. It was the start of the Arab-Israeli War, a bitterly fought conflict from which Israel emerged victorious, adding to its territory. An armistice was signed in February 1949, but the Arab countries refused to recognize Israel's right to exist.

The Israeli victory accelerated the Palestinian exodus. Many left out of fear. Some were forcibly expelled by the Israelis. Often their property was confiscated and redistributed to Israeli citizens. Between 700,000 and 1.5 million Palestinians left. By the end of 1948, only 155,000 Palestinians were left. Most of those who departed ended up in refugee camps across the borders of neighboring countries. Over the next fifty years the children who grew up in those camps would be raised to believe that Palestine—now Israel—was their homeland, and that jihad—holy war by any means necessary—was justified to reclaim it.

Chapter *3*

Making War and Making Peace

From the first, the refugee camps on Israel's borders with Syria, Lebanon, Jordan, and Egypt became flash points for violence. Palestinian fedayeen (freedom fighters) regularly raided across the border. The Israeli Army responded by attacking the camps. Both sides killed innocent civilians. The Palestinians left in Israel were often regarded as potential terrorists, and their movements were restricted.

Arab governments backed the Palestinian cause, but the refugees burdened these countries' economies and glutted their labor forces. In the camps, host nations had to provide administrative help, policing, extra food supplies, and medicine. The camps were breeding grounds for crime and disease. Frequent clashes between refugees and local residents occurred.

Opposite:
A group of anti-Israeli
fedayeen soldiers

There was lack of unity among the Arab countries and among the Palestinians. Throughout the late 1940s and 1950s, many militant factions were operating independently of each other. Lack of cohesive leadership kept them from being effective.

Nevertheless, border raids continued and tensions escalated. In October 1953, fedayeen attacked the Israeli village of Tirat Yehudah and killed a woman and her two children with grenades. An Israeli Army unit retaliated, storming into the Jordanian border town of Qibya. They demolished fifty houses and killed sixty-nine Jordanians, including women and children.

The Suez-Sinai War

There were many fedayeen raids across the Gaza Strip, a Palestinian area under Egyptian military control since the armistice halting hostilities between Egypt and Israel in 1949. Some of these raids were financed and armed by Egypt. The Palestinian refugees in the Gaza Strip were a continuing burden to Egypt, which wanted the refugees resettled in their former homeland, which was now Israel. In early 1955, Israeli forces responded to the raids, killing thirty-six soldiers and six civilians. In July 1956, Egyptian president Gamal Nasser nationalized (brought under Egyptian control) the French- and British-owned Suez Canal. Israeli shipping was barred from the canal and blockaded from the Gulf of Aqaba. In October the Israeli Army, commanded by Moshe Dayan, attacked the Gaza Strip, seized nearly all of the Sinai Peninsula, and reached the eastern bank of the canal. British planes bombed the canal region, and British and French military units invaded Egypt from the sea. Hostilities were halted by a UN resolution demanding a cease-fire.

The Israelis had killed or routed some 18,000 Egyptian soldiers and captured another 12,000.

The Six-Day War

At the end of the Suez-Sinai War in 1956, a United Nations Emergency Force (UNEF) occupied the Egyptian side of the border with Israel. In 1967, Egyptian president Nasser ordered UNEF out. He closed the Gulf of Aqaba to Israeli shipping. He then signed a pact putting the Jordanian Army under Egyptian command, and his forces massed on the Israeli border.

The Israelis struck first. On June 5, 1967, the Israeli Air Force bombed Egyptian, Syrian, Jordanian, and Iraqi airfields. More than 400 Egyptian planes were shot down by June 7. On the ground, 50 tanks were destroyed and 150 disabled. While the Israeli Army swept west across the Sinai Peninsula to the Suez Canal, paratroopers and naval units destroyed Egypt's Gulf of Aqaba blockade. On Israel's northern border, the Israeli Army overran the Golan Heights and pursued enemy forces deep into Syria.

By June 8, Jordan's army was retreating and the West Bank and Jerusalem were firmly in Israeli hands. Jewish soldiers armed with machine guns knelt in prayer at the Western Wall. Jerusalem, sacred to Muslims, Christians, and Jews alike, was no longer controlled by Jordan. Israeli defense minister Moshe Dayan exulted that "we have returned to the holiest of our holy places, never to depart from it again."

On June 10 the United Nations negotiated cease-fire agreements, and the Six-Day War ended. The Arab nations—particularly Egypt—had suffered a humiliating defeat. Israel now occupied the Sinai, the Gaza Strip, the Golan Heights, the West Bank, and Jerusalem—an area four times larger than Israel itself. However, this also brought 1,500,000 Palestinian refugees under Israeli control. They would pose a threat to internal security for more than thirty years.

Israeli soldiers stand next to the Western Wall, a sacred place in Jerusalem, which was reclaimed by Israel during the Six-Day War.

Nevertheless, the Suez Canal remained closed to Israel's shipping for the next ten years. During that time, raids and reprisals continued on the Jordanian and Syrian borders. However, a UN force stationed between Egypt and Israel prevented military encounters between them.

During the 1950s and early 1960s, the Arab countries were wracked by rebellions and civil wars. The period was also marked by the opening of productive oil fields in many Arab lands. They provided money to finance the Palestinian cause. At a meeting of the heads of the Arab nations in Egypt in 1964, the Palestine Liberation Organization (PLO), an umbrella group to coordinate anti-Israel actions, was formed.

In November 1966, responding to raids across the Jordanian border, the Israelis attacked Hebron, and a fierce battle raged. Ten days later protestors rioted against King Hussein of Jordan's policy of moderation with Israel. Reacting, Hussein began drafting men between eighteen and forty to beef up the Jordanian Army. The expanded Jordanian Army was put under Egyptian command at the beginning of the Six-Day War in June 1967.

Israel's overwhelming victory in that war resulted in the takeover of border areas used as buffer zones with hostile neighbors. A UN resolution demanded that Israel give them up. It also demanded that the Arab nations recognize Israel. When they denied recognition, Israel refused to relinquish the captured territories. Nasser threatened a new war if Israel didn't withdraw from them.

The Yom Kippur War

In March 1969, Golda Meir became prime minister, heading a Labor government. She was opposed by Israel's beloved first prime minister, David Ben-Gurion, who thought her policy of "face-to-face talks" with the

Born Goldie Mabovitch in Kiev, Russia, but raised in Milwaukee, Wisconsin, Golda Meir was always active in the Zionist cause, and became active in the Israeli government once the nation was established.

Arabs would "split the nation." Meir challenged the traditional Israeli policy toward Arabs, insisting that as long as the thinking was that "there might be a solution without negotiations, the solution is only obstructed."

Soon after she took office, there were dogfights between Israeli and Egyptian planes over the Sinai Peninsula and with Syrian jets over the Golan Heights. Syria refused to release six Israelis brought there on a hijacked airliner. The following January, Israeli planes bombed military targets in Egypt. In May, responding to repeated attacks by Palestinians across the border, Israeli forces attacked the bases of Palestinian guerrilla fighters in Lebanon, killing thirty Arabs.

Frustrated by their continued exile and conditions in the refugee camps, and blaming other countries that supported Israel, Palestinian guerrillas and their allies were responsible for many incidents during the late 1960s and 1970s. In Israel and other countries, including Italy, Greece, Sweden, Germany, and the United States, there were bombings, machine-gun attacks, assassination attempts, and hijackings. To a large extent the spread of these activities beyond the borders of Israel cost the Palestinians the sympathy of the non-Arab world.

In September 1972 at the Olympic Games in Munich, Germany, Palestinian commandos infiltrated the compound in which Israeli athletes were housed, killed two of them, and took nine others hostage. The guerrillas demanded the release of two hundred Palestinians from Israeli jails and a plane to fly them out of Germany. Although Israel refused to release any prisoners, the commandos and their hostages were flown by German helicopter to the airport to board a plane to Cairo. However, German sharpshooters opened fire on them as they emerged from the helicopters. The guerrillas fired back. When the smoke cleared, all the Palestinians and all the hostages were dead. Israel then bombed bases in Syria and Lebanon where it believed that Palestinian terrorists were being trained.

A year later, on the Jewish holy day of Yom Kippur, Egypt and Syria attacked Israel. The Israeli Army was not combat ready. However, the Israeli Air Force was able to hold off the Arab enemy—now including Jordan and Iraq—until the army rallied. During the war many Arab nations raised oil prices, reduced production, and refused to sell oil to the United States and others who backed Israel. The UN ended the Yom Kippur War after eighteen days of fighting. Egypt took back a strip of land along the east bank of the Suez Canal. Syria regained control of a small area in the Golan Heights.

A Small Move Toward Peace

As a result of the war, the Labor government fell, and Golda Meir was replaced as prime minister by Menachem Begin. A Likud hard-liner, Begin announced that Judea and Samaria were part of the ancient Jewish homeland and instituted a policy of settlement of the Israeli-occupied West Bank by Jews. The area attracted many Orthodox Jews who shared Begin's belief. Over the next few years these settlements became the focus of violence between Palestinians and Jews.

In Israel proper, there were rocket attacks on Israeli villages and bombings of beaches and of Jerusalem markets. In 1975, after the United States objected to a UN statement declaring Zionism "racist," a terrorist bomb killed fourteen people at New York's La Guardia Airport. This was followed in 1976 by the hijacking of a plane with 105 Israeli passengers aboard. The plane was landed at Entebbe Airport in Uganda, where Israeli commandos subsequently rescued the hostages.

Quite suddenly, however, in November 1977, hopes of peace were revived by an unexpected source. Anwar al-

Three Men on a Mission

In September 1978, U.S. president Jimmy Carter brought together Egyptian president Anwar al-Sadat and Israeli prime minister Menachem Begin at Camp David, Maryland, to discuss peace between their countries. During the 1940s, Begin had led the Irgun, guerrilla fighters in devastating raids against both the British and the Palestinians.. He was a Likud hard-liner firmly against making concessions to the Arabs. Sadat was the driving force behind the 1973 war against Israel.

Despite their long and bitter enmity, the Egyptians and the Israelis, worn down by the effects on their countries' economies and morale, had been trying to negotiate. However, the negotiations had broken down. "It was this stalemate, and the prospect for an even worse future," President Carter later explained, "that prompted me to invite President Sadat and Prime Minister Begin to join me at Camp David."

The two leaders were not able to negotiate face-to-face. Carter put them in separate lodges at Camp David. Then he went back and forth between them with proposals and counterproposals. This came to be known as "shuttle diplomacy."

It paid off. On September 18, 1978, Sadat and Begin signed a "Framework for the Conclusion of a Peace Treaty Between Egypt and Israel." This resulted in a formal peace treaty in 1979. They also signed a "Framework for Peace in the Middle East," which laid plans for a Palestinian homeland. Those plans, however, would be largely unrealized.

Sadat and Begin were awarded the 1978 Nobel Prize for Peace. And while Jimmy Carter's contribution was not honored, each small step toward peace in the Middle East today is a tribute to those first "shuttle diplomacy" steps taken by President Carter at Camp David.

Anwar Sadat, Jimmy Carter, and Menachem Begin relax at Camp David in Maryland.

Sadat, who had replaced Nasser as president of Egypt and organized the Yom Kippur invasion of Israel, surprised the world by visiting Israel and addressing the Knesset. After his speech, he joined hands with Prime Minister Begin to pledge "no more war!"

The leaders of the other Arab countries and the Palestinians condemned Sadat as a traitor. Talks were initiated between the Egyptians and the Israelis, but concrete solutions proved more difficult than good intentions. Good feelings between Sadat and Begin were short-lived. The talks broke down.

It would be a year before U.S. president Jimmy Carter revived the peace process by bringing Sadat and Begin to Camp David, Maryland. Here an agreement was hammered out for a peace treaty between the two countries. The Palestinian question, however, remained no closer to a peaceful solution than it had been.

Chapter 4

The Road to Oslo

Between 1977 and 1988, the Likud government settled 60,000 Jews on the West Bank. When the local Palestinians objected, they were met with an "iron fist" policy that included shutting off the water supply and electricity, the razing of houses, and imprisonment without trial. The Palestinians retaliated by harassing the settlers, sometimes with sniper fire.

The first of many problems that the Israeli government would have with Jewish settlers was in 1982, when the peace treaty with Egypt required some of them to leave their villages. They fought pitched battles with Israeli troops. The settlers in Yamat threatened collective suicide. They were forcibly removed, and the town was bulldozed to prevent their return.

Opposite:
In 1982, Israel responded in kind to fundamentalist Muslim raids across its borders by invading Lebanon with tanks and airplanes, causing heavy losses and widespread damage.

Likud and Lebanon

Likud pursued a hard-line policy internationally. In 1981, Israeli F-4 Phantom jets destroyed an Iraqi nuclear reactor with so-called smart bombs. The raids brought protests from many countries, including the United States, but Prime Minister Begin claimed that the reactor would have enabled Iraq to drop nuclear bombs on Israel. At the same time, Israel warned that it now could make nuclear bombs itself.

Arab governments viewed this as a threat, which also fueled their anger against Sadat for making peace with Israel. Among the Arab nations, Egypt was isolated and Sadat was a pariah. On October 6, 1981, he was assassinated while reviewing an army parade in Cairo. His murderers were Muslim fundamentalists opposed to peace with Israel.

Other Muslim fundamentalists were in Lebanon, where the PLO had relocated. Brutal raids on Israeli towns across the border were frequent, claiming many innocent victims. Finally Israel reacted, and in June 1982, 20,000 soldiers and hundreds of tanks backed up by planes invaded southern Lebanon. PLO forces and their Syrian allies in Lebanon suffered heavy losses.

Both members of the Knesset and other nations protested the incursion. But Begin stood firm, and on July 27, Israeli jets dropped cluster bombs on West Beirut, killing 120 and wounding 232—most of them civilians—in violation of a U.S.-Israel treaty banning such weapons. More than 100,000 young Israelis demonstrated against the war in Lebanon—"the first sign of a substantial peace movement" in Israel.

On September 18, Israeli troops sealed off Sabra and Shatila, two Palestinian refugee camps in Lebanon. Phalangists—Christian militia allied with the Israelis—entered the camps and slaughtered more than a thousand

Likud and Labor: The Major Parties

Although the two major political parties in Israel are Labor and Likud, when in office they rule as leaders of a coalition. The present coalition led by Prime Minister Ehud Barak's One Israel party (the renamed Labor party) consists of seven parties. It controls 75 seats of the 120-seat Knesset.

The Labor party began in 1948 as the Mapai party, led by David Ben-Gurion. In 1968, Mapai merged with two other parties to form the Labor party. It stood for Zionist-Socialist principles, unlimited immigration, the rights of labor, and a strong defense. It opposed demands to impose Chasidic law, stood firm against Arab aggression, and until 1977 sanctioned Jewish settlements in conquered territories.

That year the Herut (Freedom party) formed alliances to organize the Likud party. Demanding permanent control of the West Bank and Jerusalem, Likud gained wide support among settlers and Orthodox Israelis who claimed a biblical right to these areas. Likud also was popular among non-European Israelis who saw Labor as elitist. In 1977, Likud ousted Labor, and Menachem Begin became prime minister.

In 1984, Likud's shaky Knesset majority forced it into a coalition with Labor. However, the coalition collapsed in 1990 because of disagreements over the Middle East peace process. In 1992, Labor was voted back in with Yitzhak Rabin as prime minister. Following Rabin's assassination in 1995, Likud's Benjamin Netanyahu narrowly won election as prime minister. For four years, he delayed implementing the Oslo Peace Accords negotiated under Rabin. Peace was still the issue in 1999, when Barak ousted Netanyahu, putting Labor back in power. And so the seesaw battle to mold Israel's future continues.

people, most of them unarmed, and "many of them," according to newspaper reports, "elderly men, women, and children." In 1983 an Israeli government commission found that Defense Minister Ariel Sharon shared responsibility for the massacre, and he was forced to resign.

As Israel's main supporter and supplier of armaments, the United States was blamed for Israeli acts of violence. Also in 1983, the U.S. Embassy in Beirut was bombed by the Vengeance Organization of Sabra and Shatila Martyrs—one of many guerrilla groups operating independently of the PLO. Forty people were killed. A suicide bombing of the U.S. Marine barracks in Beirut later that year resulted in 246 deaths.

The *Achille Lauro* Hijacking

Menachem Begin stepped down in September 1983, and Yitzhak Shamir became head of the Likud government. Attacks against U.S. installations and citizens in Lebanon continued. But it was the October 1985 hijacking of the cruise ship *Achille Lauro* that escalated American outrage against Palestinian terrorists. They seized the vessel as it left Alexandria, Egypt, with more than sixty American tourists on board. One of the hijackers shot and killed Leon Klinghoffer, an elderly Jewish American in a wheelchair. His physical condition prevented him from resisting, let alone posing a threat to the hijackers. His murder became a symbol of the danger that Palestinians posed to Jews and Americans everywhere.

The hijackers demanded the release of Palestinian prisoners held by Israel. When their demands weren't met, they surrendered to the Egyptian government. They were to be given safe passage to Tunisia. However, U.S. Navy jets forced their plane to land in Italy, where their leader escaped and the other hijackers later stood trial.

The *Intifada*

In 1987, living conditions in Palestinian refugee camps and villages were deplorable. Water supply and sewage systems were inadequate. The roads were ungraded and unpaved. The high Palestinian birthrate had resulted in overcrowding and poverty. Jobs were scarce and involved long hours of traveling. Often the Israeli Army closed the roads, and the Palestinians couldn't get to work. This added to their poverty—and to their spirit of rebellion.

At this time a fundamentalist revival was attracting Palestinians in Israel and the occupied territories. The core of the revival was a religious claim to an "Islamic Palestine." Young people impatient with the PLO were inspired by an Islamic appeal that transcended politics.

Their impatience exploded in 1987. In the Gaza Strip, the West Bank, and Jerusalem, hordes of young Arabs flung rocks at Israeli soldiers. Led by teenagers, the rock throwers included children as young as eight and nine years of age. Many of them had been inspired by the teachings in schools run by Islamic fundamentalists where they had been told that the occupied territories were Islamic holy ground.

The young people stormed the headquarters of Israeli police forces. They overran Jewish settlements and army roadblocks. In Jerusalem they attacked Israeli banks. "We want any means of getting back at the Jews," one of them said. When the soldiers defended themselves with rifle fire and children were killed, Palestinian adults—men and women—joined the *intifada.*

According to the Israeli human rights organization B'Tselem, 1,346 Palestinians, including 276 children, were killed by Israeli soldiers during the *intifada.* Palestinians killed 127 soldiers and 256 civilians. It lasted for six years, subsiding when the Oslo Peace Accords were reached in 1993.

A symbol of the *intifada*: A young Palestinian boy carries ammunition—rocks and a bottle—to do his part to take back Islamic holy ground.

Palestinian violence, both by the PLO and terrorist anti-PLO fanatics whose goal was vengeance rather than simply discussing their differences, was now occurring around the world. Tourists at the El Al Airlines counters in the Rome and Vienna airports were killed by grenades and submachine guns. A bomb killed four passengers aboard a TWA airliner bound for Athens, Greece. A discotheque frequented by American servicemen in Berlin was rocked by an explosion killing 2 and wounding 155. Bombs were found in luggage at London's Heathrow Airport. In Istanbul, 21 people praying in a synagogue were killed by Arab terrorists. Palestinian bomb attacks in Paris killed 13 people. Every week brought new incidents.

There was also escalation in Israel and the occupied territories. In 1987 the *intifada* (young people's uprising) erupted. On a daily basis Israeli police and army troops found themselves facing unprecedented violence. For the first time, Palestinians in Israel were emulating protestors in the occupied territories and confronting the authorities. During that first year demonstrations increased from five hundred per year to three thousand. Some 2.1 million Palestinians, said one analyst, "are in the first stages of a civil uprising."

Encouraged by the *intifada*, in November 1988 the PLO declared that an independent state of Palestine existed. Israel rejected the declaration. Led by Hamas, some militant factions split off from the PLO in protest against its moderation. They vowed to step up terrorism in Israel and abroad. This fueled the *intifada*, and by 1990, Palestinian militants were killing Palestinians who cooperated with Israelis. Battling the *intifada*, the Israelis shot demonstrators and escalated their policy of jailing Arab suspects without trial, expelling people from their villages, and destroying their houses.

A Promise of Peace

The situation seemed hopeless, and then—suddenly—there was hope. In 1992, Israelis elected a Labor party government headed by Yitzhak Rabin as prime minister. That December a secret meeting took place in London between Israelis and the PLO. It was followed by fourteen secret sessions of negotiations in Oslo, Norway, over a period of eight months. By August 1993 the participants had drafted and revised a peace agreement. On September 13, 1993, in Washington, D.C., President Clinton stood between Yitzhak Rabin and PLO chairman Yasir Arafat as the Oslo Accords were signed.

President Bill Clinton watches as Israeli prime minister Yitzhak Rabin (left) and Yasir Arafat shake hands during the signing of the 1993 Oslo Accords.

The accords granted the Palestinians five years of limited self-rule in the Gaza Strip and the West Bank in exchange for ceasing hostilities against Israel. Palestinians would have the right to hold elections and create their own government. A Palestinian police force would replace Israeli soldiers, but the Israeli Army would guard Jewish settlements within the territories and patrol borders and major roads. A joint committee would be set up to settle disputes. Israel would help with economic development of the transferred lands.

There would be ongoing negotiations on unresolved issues during the five-year period. These included the degree of Palestinian self-rule, the question of complete independence for the Palestinian state, defining its borders, the fate of Jerusalem, the ingathering of refugee Palestinians from Arab nations, the fate of Jewish settlements inside the Palestinian-controlled areas, the fate of Palestinian territories still under Israeli rule, and other matters.

Even as the exchange of control began on the West Bank, militant Palestinians and hard-line Israeli settlers opposed the agreement. Nevertheless, the first Palestinian election resulted in the al-Fatah wing of the PLO capturing 75 percent of the seats in a new Palestinian parliament and Yasir Arafat being named president in 1996. Within eight months he would face a major test of his ability to restrain Palestinian rage.

Murder of a Peacemaker

During the Muslim holy month of Ramadan in 1994, worshipers gathered to pray at the Haram al-Ibrahimi mosque in Hebron, when Baruch Goldstein entered brandishing a Galil automatic assault rifle. He fired 118 shots and threw three grenades, killing twenty-nine Muslims and wounding hundreds more. In the days fol-

An Israeli soldier stands guard at the grave of Baruch Goldstein.

lowing the killings there were riots in Hebron that resulted in Israeli soldiers shooting and killing 24 more Palestinians.

Most Israelis regarded Goldstein as a lunatic and a madman. He had been a follower of the American-Jewish extremist Meir Kahane, who believed all non-Jews should be forcibly expelled from Israel. After Goldstein's death, his grave became a shrine to fanatic Jewish settlers.

Some of these settlers belonged to a right-wing group called Eyal. Many in the group regarded Baruch Goldstein as a hero. Yigal Amir, a law student from the town of Herzliyah, had ties to Eyal. He believed the Oslo Accords were a betrayal of Israel. On November 4, 1995, in King's Square in Tel Aviv, Amir gunned down Yitzhak Rabin as he was leaving a peace rally he had addressed. The seventy-three-year-old prime minister died of his wounds. Nine days later, Israeli troops began to withdraw from the West Bank as agreed to in the Oslo Accords.

Roadblocks to Peace

In March 1996, four Palestinian terrorist attacks in Israel took sixty-two lives, and Arafat was subsequently blamed for not controlling Palestinian militants. Israeli voters turned against the accords and the Labor party. As a result, the Likud gained a narrow victory in the June 1996 elections. Likud also owed its success to alliances with ultra-Orthodox parties seeking to make their religious practices a matter of Israeli law.

The new prime minister was Benjamin Netanyahu, who strongly opposed the land-for-peace accords. Although he had promised to live up to them during the election campaign, once in office he balked. He cited Palestinian terrorism as the reason. The new Palestinian National Authority replied that his reneging was the cause of the terrorist acts.

Netanyahu authorized new Jewish settlements in the West Bank and objected to returning the Golan Heights to Syria. He also delayed pulling Israeli troops out of Hebron and postponed their staged withdrawal from the West Bank. Netanyahu then suspended talks with Arafat and declared that Israel would never agree to an independent Palestine. He said he wanted to renegotiate some terms of the Oslo Accords, but as expected, Arafat refused.

In September 1996, Netanyahu authorized the excavation of an archaeological tunnel leading to the Temple Mount in Jerusalem, one of Islam's holiest sites. Jerusalem Muslims protested this as a sacrilege and rioted. The demonstrations spread to other Palestinian areas. Dozens were killed and hundreds wounded in the clashes that followed.

The Israelis surrounded Palestinian cities with tanks and set up barricades. Roads were closed, cutting links between 450 villages and barring Palestinians from getting to work. The Palestinian economy was stifled. More and more Palestinians were wondering if the militants were right in calling Arafat "an Israeli pawn."

An October 1996 poll found that 80 percent of Israelis favored honoring the Oslo Accords, and that 57 percent thought Netanyahu was mishandling things. More than 50,000 Tel Aviv peace activists demonstrated against his policies. The nations of the world also wanted peace. They pressured Netanyahu and Arafat to meet at the Wye Plantation in Maryland.

The Fall of Netanyahu

At Wye, the Oslo Accords were affirmed. Netanyahu agreed to withdraw occupation forces from 13 percent of the West Bank in return for guarantees of Israeli security. However, Zionist settlers felt there could be no security.

The last part of Benjamin Netanyahu's term as prime minister was plagued by violence on all sides, a weakened economy, and a rising unemployment rate.

When they demonstrated against the Wye agreement, Netanyahu placated them by announcing that there would be no more land-for-peace exchanges. The Palestinians were furious, and the United States government accused Netanyahu of betraying the Wye agreement.

Throughout 1997 and 1998, the violence continued. During the five years following the signing of the Oslo Accords, more Israelis were killed by Palestinian terrorists than in the fifteen previous years. A total of 279 men, women, and children died in 92 terrorist attacks.

By 1999, Israel's economy was in trouble with a declining growth rate of 1.9 percent. The unemployment rate was 10 percent and rising. The poor were discontented and fearful. Working-class Jews feared that peace with Palestinians would create an influx of cheap Arab labor, which would lower their living standards. In 1998, 21.8 percent of the nation's children were living below the poverty line. Among the poorest of the poor were Ethiopian Jews, who rioted, claiming they were discriminated against.

Finally, the Knesset moved to dissolve the Likud government and hold new elections. There were immediate moves within the Likud to seize control of the party by anti-Netanyahu candidates who were more harshly opposed to the peace process than even he had been. Thirty-five parties participated in the election for the Knesset, and five major candidates were presented for prime minister. On New Year's Day 1999, the *Jerusalem Post* predicted that the nation's choice would "be between anarchy and dictatorship."

It didn't turn out quite like that. Although fifteen parties were elected to the Knesset, three of the candidates for prime minister dropped out of the race at the last minute. Labor—now restructured as the One Israel party—regained control of the government with Ehud Barak as prime minister. He was firmly committed to the peace process.

Chapter 5

Ongoing Issues for Israelis and Palestinians

Prime Minister Barak and President Arafat continue their slow, stop-start movement toward peace. So far their success must be measured in frustratingly small steps rather than final goals. The steps are important, but so, too, are the problems not yet resolved.

Land for peace is still a key issue. How much land? How much peace? What will happen to the land that is traded? What will happen to the Jewish settlers who live on it? How will the Palestinians and Israelis arrive at a fair distribution of water in those areas where water is scarce?

Can Arafat's Palestinian National Authority really guarantee peace? Has it the power to stop terrorist attacks? Has it the will? In Hebron, Ramallah, and

Opposite:
A female Israeli soldier looks down from the Golan Heights to the Sea of Galilee in January 2000. Israel captured this area from Syria during the Six-Day War in 1967.

Nablus, protests against Israel's not releasing Palestinian prisoners resulted in riots and exchanges of gunfire between Israeli soldiers and Palestinian Authority police. As a result, peace talks between Israelis and Palestinians were temporarily broken off, and the process of land-for-peace exchanges was halted.

Other major issues may not be addressed for some time. Will the Palestinians be granted a state completely independent of Israeli authority? How will the question of Jerusalem—claimed by both Israelis and Palestinians as their capital—be settled? How will the matter of release for Palestinian prisoners convicted of killing Israelis be resolved?

In February 2000, the peace process suffered major setbacks. Angered by what they saw as stalling on the transfer of West Bank territory, the Palestinians broke off peace talks with Israel on other major issues. At the same time, Syria and Israel were unable to reach an agreement on just how much territory would be relinquished to Syria when the Israeli occupation of the Golan Heights was ended. Shortly after the negotiations collapsed, Hezbollah guerrillas—believed to be under the control of Syria—attacked Israelis across the Lebanese border. The Israelis responded with bombing raids on Lebanese cities. The raids continued even as it was rumored that contacts were being made between the Israelis and the Palestinians in an effort to restart the peace talks.

Three months later Israel evacuated the buffer area with Lebanon. The question is, will the Syrian-influenced Hezbollah resume across-the-border raids on Israeli communities? With Syria and Israel at an impasse over the return of the Golan Heights, how will the possibility of raids from Lebanon affect the peace process in general?

Each of the leaders has problems within his own ranks. Arafat must deal with many competing demands by those under his rule, those still in the occupied territories, those in the refugee camps, and even those who are Israeli citizens. He is criticized by some Palestinians every time his forces arrest terrorists and turn them over to the Israelis. The criticism is exploited by Muslim fundamentalists in the refugee camps who use it as a propaganda tool to enlist young people in the battle against the peace process. Contrarily, many West Bank and Israeli Palestinians are clamoring for Arafat to take more effective action against terrorists who have been killing fellow Palestinians for collaborating with Israel.

One of the PLO demands has always been for the readmission of exiled Palestinians to the lands they fled. Israel has always opposed this, and still does. Now, however, Palestinian laborers in the Gaza Strip are opposing readmission because they fear that an influx of workers competing for scarce jobs might deprive them of their livelihood.

Barak also must deal with domestic problems. Like the Gaza Strip Palestinians, Sephardic Israelis, who have a low standard of living, fear the effects of an influx of low-wage Palestinians on the economy. They continue to protest a class system weighted in favor of newly arrived Russian immigrants. Barak is caught between the two groups' constant conflicts over lifestyle, roots, and religion.

Shas is becoming more and more of a factor in this struggle. Its seventeen seats in the Knesset continue to give Shas the power to decide close votes. As they solidify Sephardic support, they continue to clash with Barak's government over the financing of religion and the integrating of ultra-Orthodox ideology into Israeli law. If Barak gives in to Shas, he risks losing secular support for his peace efforts. However, if he does not meet some of their demands, he risks their resignation from the coalition that pushes his peace initiatives through the Knesset.

Adding to Barak's problems are demands by the business community that he speed up the peace process. At the same time, they want him to put down Palestinian terrorism without using the kind of harsh measures that stain Israel's image in the eyes of potential international investors. They constantly remind him that images of the *intifada* scared away foreign investment, and that was very bad for the Israeli economy.

As serious as the situation is, all these problems are solvable if there is the will to solve them. Although history in the Middle East is written day by day, in the long term there is survival for both Palestinians and Jews. They have been living together in the region—sometimes in peace, sometimes not—for many thousands of years. A new millennium is just one more challenge in an ancient land with an unlimited supply of time. Time is always on the side of peace.

Chronology

8000 B.C.	First settlements of farmers and sheep- and goat-herding nomads evolve in Canaan (later known as Palestine/Israel).
1500 B.C.	First Hebrew tribes settle in Canaan.
1000 B.C.	Establishment of Kingdom of Israel
ca.64 B.C.	Rome conquers the region.
A.D. 1	Arabic civilization begins to take hold among non-Jews in Palestine.
70	Romans destroy Jerusalem, the Hebrews' holiest city.
132	Romans kill more than half a million Jewish men.
613	Muhammad begins preaching new religion of Islam to followers called Muslims.
641	Arabs conquer Palestine, drive out the Romans, and begin the spread of Islam. First exodus of Jews follows.
1099	European Crusaders conquer Palestine. Second exodus of Jews follows.
1100–1900	Anti-Semitism drives Jews from country to country in Europe.
1600s	Ottoman Empire (Turkey) conquers Palestine and occupies it until 1917.
1897	The First Zionist Congress convenes in Basel, Switzerland.
1903	The anti-Semitic but influential *Protocols of the Learned Elders of Zion* is published.
1917	During World War I, the British drive the Turks out of Palestine and promise the Palestinians an independent state.
1917 (Nov. 2)	The British issue the Balfour Declaration, supporting Zionist claims in Palestine.
1922	League of Nations approves British rule over Palestine.
1936–1939	Civil War between Jews and Palestinians
1939	The British issue White Paper limiting Jewish immigration to Palestine and promising to establish an independent Palestinian state with an Arab majority.
1939–1945	Six million Jews perish in the Holocaust.
1947	Following repeated clashes between Zionists and the British over illegal immigration, the UN divides Palestine into Jewish and Palestinian states. Palestinians reject the plan.
1948 (May 14)	Nation of Israel is pro-claimed under the leader-

ship of Prime Minister David Ben-Gurion. Arab nations invade and are defeated by Israelis.

1949 — Palestinian refugee camps are established on both sides of Israel's borders with Egypt, Jordan, Lebanon, and Syria.

1956 — Egypt nationalizes Suez Canal; Israel, France, and England invade Egypt; UN imposes a cease-fire.

1964 — Palestine Liberation Organization (PLO) is formed.

1967 — Winning of Six-Day War results in Israel occupying the Golan Heights, Sinai Peninsula, Gaza Strip, West Bank, and Jerusalem.

1969 — Golda Meir is elected prime minister of Israel.

1973 — Yom Kippur War (Israel vs. Egypt and Syria) results in heavy Israeli casualties and is blamed on Meir. She is forced out of office.

1977 — Egyptian president Anwar al-Sadat visits Jerusalem, addresses Knesset.

1978 — Camp David Accords foreshadowing a peace treaty between Israel and Egypt are signed.

1981 (Oct. 6) — Sadat is assassinated by Egyptian fundamentalists opposed to peace with Israel.

1982 — Israel invades Lebanon.

1987 — The *intifada,* an ongoing rebellion against Israeli occupation, begins in the West Bank and Gaza Strip.

1992 — Yitzhak Rabin is elected Israeli prime minister. Secret peace talks with the Palestinians begin.

1993 (Sept. 13) — The Oslo Peace Accords are signed by Rabin and Arafat in Washington, D.C.

1994 — Baruch Goldstein slaughters Muslims at prayer in a Hebron mosque.

1995 (Nov. 4) — Rabin is assassinated by Yigal Amir, an Israeli opponent of the Oslo Peace Accords.

1996 — Yasir Arafat is elected first president of the Palestinian National Authority.

1996 (March) — Four Palestinian terrorist attacks in Israel take sixty-two lives.

1996 (June) — Benjamin Netanyahu is elected Israeli prime minister. He suspends talks with Arafat and halts withdrawal of troops called for in the Oslo Accords.

1996 (October) — Netanyahu and Arafat sign the Wye peace agreement in Maryland. Within weeks the United States government accuses Netanyahu of reneging on it.

1999 (May 17) — Netanyahu is ousted and Ehud Barak is elected Israeli prime minister.

1999 — Peace schedule begins to be implemented; land is transferred to the Palestinian Authority; Palestinian prisoners are released; a "safe passage" route is opened between the Gaza Strip and the West Bank.

For Further Reading

Ferber, Elizabeth. *Yasir Arafat: A Life of War and Peace.* Brookfield, CT: The Millbrook Press, 1995.

Fink, Ida. *Traces (Stories of the Holocaust).* New York: Henry Holt and Company, 1998.

Ganeri, Anita. *I Remember Palestine.* Chatham, NJ: Raintree Steck-Vaughn, 1994.

Mack, Stanley. *The Story of the Jews: A 4,000-Year Adventure.* New York: Villard Books, 1998.

Mozeson, I. E., and Lois Stavsky. *Jerusalem Mosaic: Voices from the Holy City.* New York: Simon and Schuster, 1994.

Ong, Cathryn J. *The Middle East in Search of Peace* (Updated Edition). Brookfield, CT: The Millbrook Press, 1996.

Orlev, Uri. *Lydia, Queen of Palestine* (Fiction). New York: Houghton Mifflin Company, 1993.

Sawyer, Kem Knapp. *Refugees.* Springfield, NJ: Enslow Publishers, Inc., 1995.

Schlesinger, Arthur M., Jr. and Fred L. Israel, eds. *Jerusalem & the Holy Land: Chronicles from National Geographic.* Broomall, PA: Chelsea House Publishers, 1999.

Index